BYGONE

MARKET HARBOROUGH

© 1982
Anderson Publications
Blaby, Leicester

Printed by A.B. Printers Ltd, Leicester

Contents

Streets	Page 5
Plan of Market Harborough, 1776	9
Occasions	17
Old Advertisements	20
The Bowdens	22
St. Mary in Arden	25
Markets	27
Transport	31
At Work	35

Acknowledgements

The author wishes to express his gratitude to all who kindly gave permission to reproduce illustrations and maps; Birmingham Reference Library for items from the Stone Collection, Mr J.H. Brown, Mr F. Herbert, the Leicester Mercury, the Leicestershire Museums, Art Galleries and Records Service, Mr H.R. Martin, the Motor Cycle, Mr H.M. Saunders, R.& W.H. Symington, Mr E. Tooms, Mr L. Wallis and Mr H.W. Webb.

The Parish Church of St Dionysius. The lofty 154 foot steeple is a particularly fine example of the stonemason's art.

Front Cover: Market stalls by the Old Grammar School. Mr Smyth's building instructions said that the school was 'to be built to stand upon posts or columns over part of the Market Place to keep the market people dry in times of foul weather'.

Streets

The Square from the High Street. Messrs Church's corn merchants former shop is on the right

Trades in the town have included coopers, glovers, a rope maker, hop merchants, brick and tile makers, dyers, a gunsmith, curriers, straw hat makers and millers.

The central High Street with the road occupied soley by the two post office workers pushing their hand cart.

On the left is the Hind Hotel, then James Barnsley's tailor, hatter, etc at the Old Bank House, and after the bank Eatons ironmongers shop. Further along is Steven's Garage

Many of the older properties in the High Street have long, narrow cramped yards behind formed by the sub division of the width of the original tofts and crofts. These were land holdings with a house fronting the street and outhouses behind with a small pasture for animals — the croft.

The town as seen from the air in the early 30's.

1 Logan Street factory
2 Coventry Road
3 Tannery, The Commons
4 Cattle Market
5 Northampton Road river bridge
6 Retail market on the Square

7 St Mary's Road
8 R. & W.H. Symington's factory
9 Burnmill Road
10 Park House
Between the Church and no. 8 lies Sun Yard
demolished to make space for Roman Way.

Looking across floods in Coventry Road towards Wood's shop and Symington's 'old side' factory. Formerly a carpet works consisting of three floors it was enlarged by the addition of three more. Flooding presented problems in the town for many years but this hazard has gradually been alleviated. It is recorded that on St Swithain's Day, 1880 water stood three feet deep inside the Parish Church and ten feet deep on the Square. Other areas such as Springfield Street suffered too and railway travellers would keep above the waters by walking home from the station along the railway embankments.

Legend to map

1. Protestant Dissenters Meeting House and Burial Ground.
2. House purchased for the residence of the Minister for the time being.
3. Free School founded by Mr Robert Smyth.
4. Guard House.
5. Quakers Meeting House and Burial Ground.
6. House belonging to the Master of the Free School for the time being.
7. Parsonage House.
8. Antinomian Meeting House.

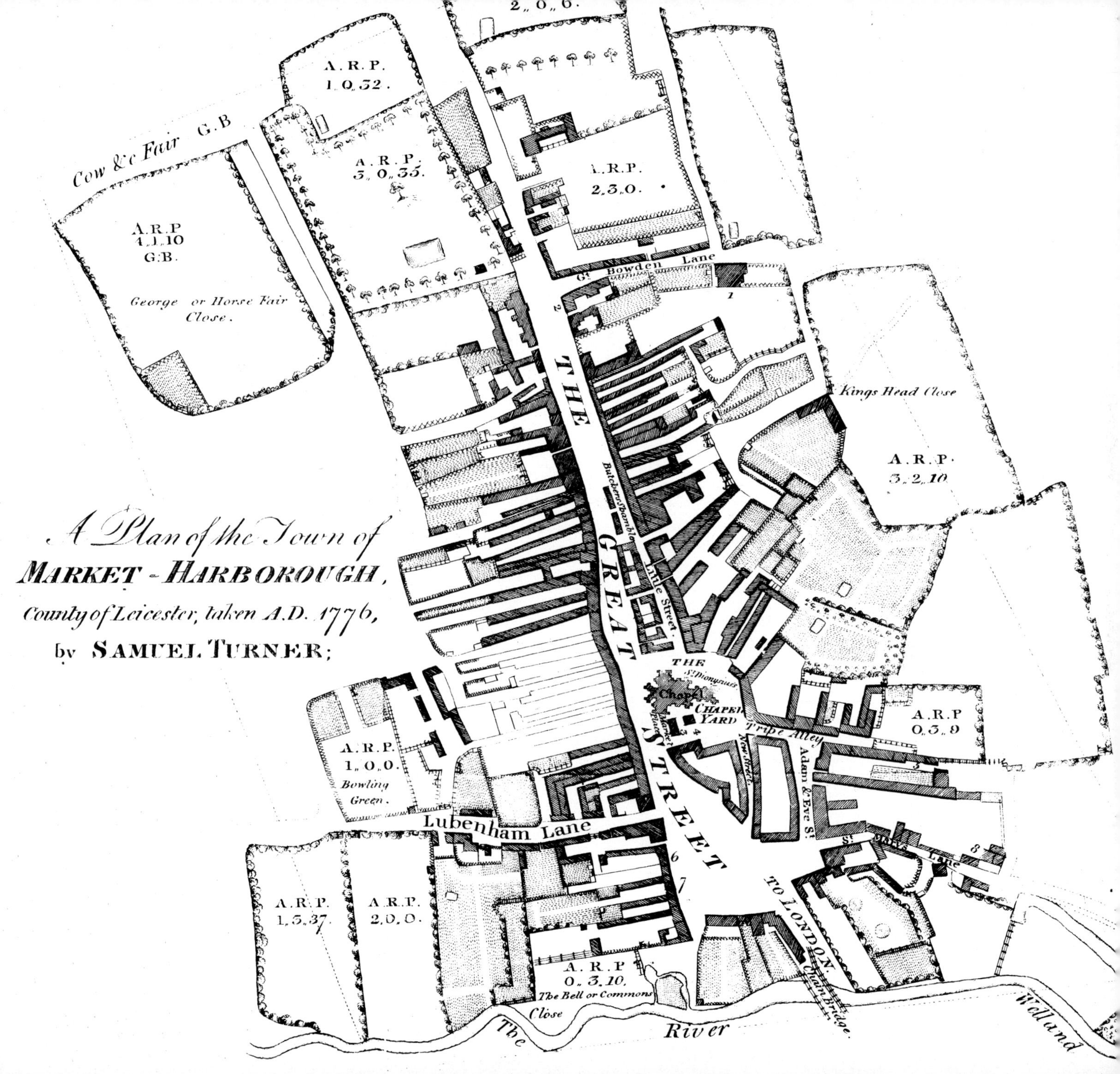

2,,0,,6.
Cow &c Fair G.B
A.R.P. 1,0,32.
A.R.P. 3,,0,,35.
A.R.P. 2,3,,0.
A.R.P 4,1,,10 G.B.
George or Horse Fair Close.
Gt Bowden Lane
1
2
Kings Head Close
A.R.P 3,,2,,10
THE GREAT STREET
Butchers Shambles
Little Street
A Plan of the Town of
MARKET - HARBOROUGH,
County of Leicester, taken A.D. 1776,
by SAMUEL TURNER;
THE St Dionysius Chapel
Market Place
CHAPEL YARD
4
Tripe Alley
New Street
Adam & Eve St.
A.R.P 0,3,,9
3
A.R.P. 1,0,0.
Bowling Green.
Lubenham Lane
5
6
7
St Marys Lane
8
TO LONDON.
A.R.P. 1,3,37.
A.R.P. 2,0,0.
A.R.P. 0,,3,10.
The Bell or Commons Close
Chain Bridge.
The River Welland

Market Place, Market Harborough

St Mary's Road from the Square. The attractive marble drinking water fountain with horse trough was moved from the position shown to Church Square.

On the left is the Cock Inn and next to it the Old Crown with the Peacock, formerly the Mermaid on the right. Many inns have existed in the town and have included the following: on the east side of High Street the Horse & Trumpet, Red Lion, Duke of Wellington, Shoulder of Mutton, Three Crowns, Axe & Cleaver, Kings Head, and on the west side the Ram, Coach & Horses, Vine, Peale (Hind), George, Saracens Head and White Hart.

The High Street from the Square with the Coffee House on the left and Emersons on the right.

Looking from Church Square towards Adam and Eve Street c.1880 before the area on the left was demolished to make way for an extension to R. & W.H. Symington's corset factory. In more recent times a further expansion to the works replaced the Dolphin Inn and other property in Factory Lane, on the right.

Taken in 1885, the original copy of this photograph is marked 'Back entrance to the town' and refers to the Back Road now known as Fairfield Road.

The High Street decorated with flags in 1911 for King George V's coronation. Mawer and Saunders ironmongers shop originated in Adam and Eve Street in 1902 and moved to its present site in 1909. Note the handcart for delivery of goods and the large area of cobble stones.

St Mary's Road with W.H. Smith's bookshop on the left and Mill Hill Road on the right at the top of which stood one of the towns two windmills, the other being near to Leicester Road on high ground opposite the Wooden Bridge.

EASTMANS
MAWER & SAUNDERS
MAWER & SAUNDERS
ROOFING SHEETS FROM
M. TOMALIN & SON
DYERS & DRY CLEANERS
M. TOMALIN & SON
DYERS & DRY CLEANERS
GENTS SUITS CLEANED FROM
CORONATION LAMPS
PAPER WA
THE CENTRAL DINING ROOM
A. JOHNSON
MANCHESTER & BRADFORD WAREHOUSE
THE WAREHOUSE

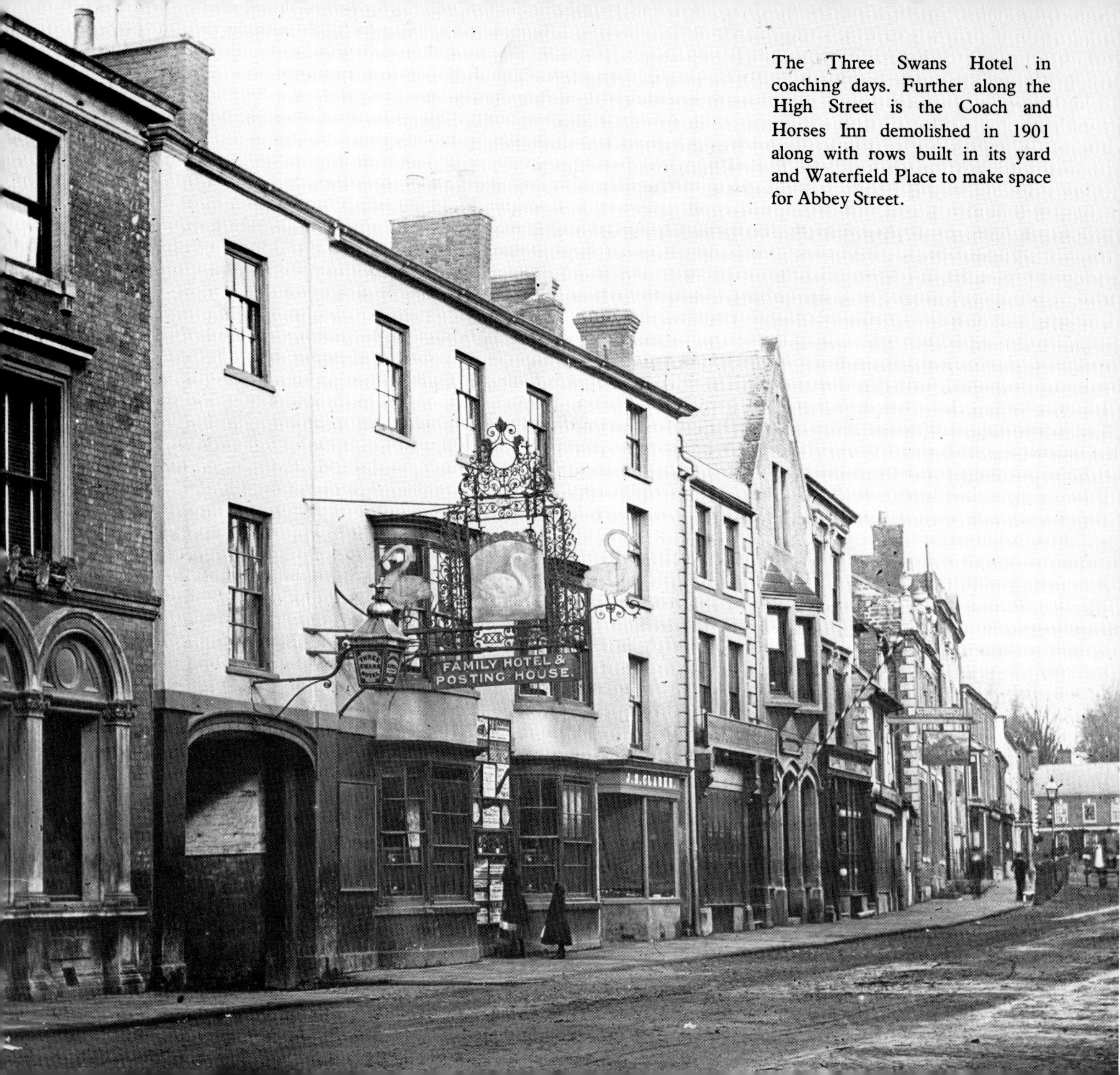

The Three Swans Hotel in coaching days. Further along the High Street is the Coach and Horses Inn demolished in 1901 along with rows built in its yard and Waterfield Place to make space for Abbey Street.

Leicester Road in 1908. The lack of people on many of these old pictures is quite striking and is possibly due to the photographers deliberately choosing a quiet period to suit the long exposure times required.

Northampton Road before narrowing by the addition of verges. The Symington brothers came to the town from Nithsdale in Scotland, hence the name for Nithsdale Avenue on the left. Following the closure of the railway the bridge across the road has been removed.

Preparing to celebrate the relief of Mafeking by a parade through the town. May 1900.

Occasions

Due to the nuisance of holding markets and fairs in the streets when upwards of two thousand beasts were in the town, the Council purchased the Market Rights and constructed a purpose built market off the streets. Mr Speight, whose photographic studio was on the Square, recorded in this picture the opening of the market in April 1903 at its Northampton Road entrance. The Brewery is on the left and on the right, buildings used in the 1800's by Mr Newham for coach manufacture.

The first Armistice Day Service around the war memorial, attended
by a good part of the town's population.

School children passing by Green's shop
on their way to play a game of cricket.

Old Advertisements

Shindlers shop faced the Square.

Church's shop stood in the high street opposite the church.

Haddon Buswell.

Complete House Furnisher,

Furniture Remover .
and Warehouseman.

Upholsterer, Cabinet Maker & Undertaker.

Carpets.
Linoleums.
Overmantels.
Sideboards.

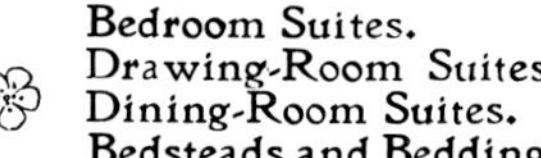

Bedroom Suites.
Drawing-Room Suites.
Dining-Room Suites.
Bedsteads and Bedding.

8, High Street, Market Harborough.

F. G. Shindler,

**Everything in Drapery for
LADIES' and CHILDREN'S WEAR.**

DEPARTMENTS.

DRESSES.	UMBRELLAS.	MANTLES.
SILKS & VELVETS.	GLOVES.	COSTUMES.
LINENS	HABERDASHERY.	UNDER—
CALICOES.	TRIMMINGS.	CLOTHING.
LACES.	SEWING—	HOSIERY.
RIBBONS.	MACHINES.	CARPETS.
FURS.	MILLINERY.	LINOLEUM.

DRESSMAKING.

LONDON HOUSE,
Market Harborough.

Telegrams :
" Church. Market Harborough.''

Telephone
0186.

CHURCH & SON

MARKET HARBOROUGH,

*Corn, Cake & complete Forage
Merchants.*

**The Oldest-Established Business
of this description in the district.**

High-Class Forage for
Hunters a Speciality.

Horses contracted for by the week.

BEST OLD OATS,	COTTON CAKES,
,, ,, HAY,	ROBSON'S FEED
STRAW,	CAKES,
PEAT MOSS,	LAMB FOOD,
BRAN,	BARLEY MEAL,
PEAS,	SHARPS,
BEANS,	MAIZE, Etc.,
DOG BISCUITS,	SALT.
LINSEED CAKES,	

MOLASSINE MEAL & CONDIMENTS.

———— **At close Market Prices.** ————

The Bowdens

The Little Bowden parish church of St. Nicholas which at one time had a wooden tower.

The course of the river has been altered since this picture was taken in about 1920.

Floods by the Cherry Tree Inn seen on the right. The other property, Latimer House, was demolished to allow the main Kettering Road to be widened.

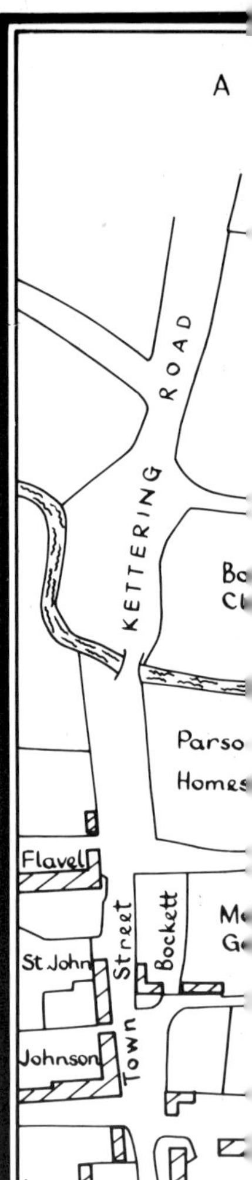

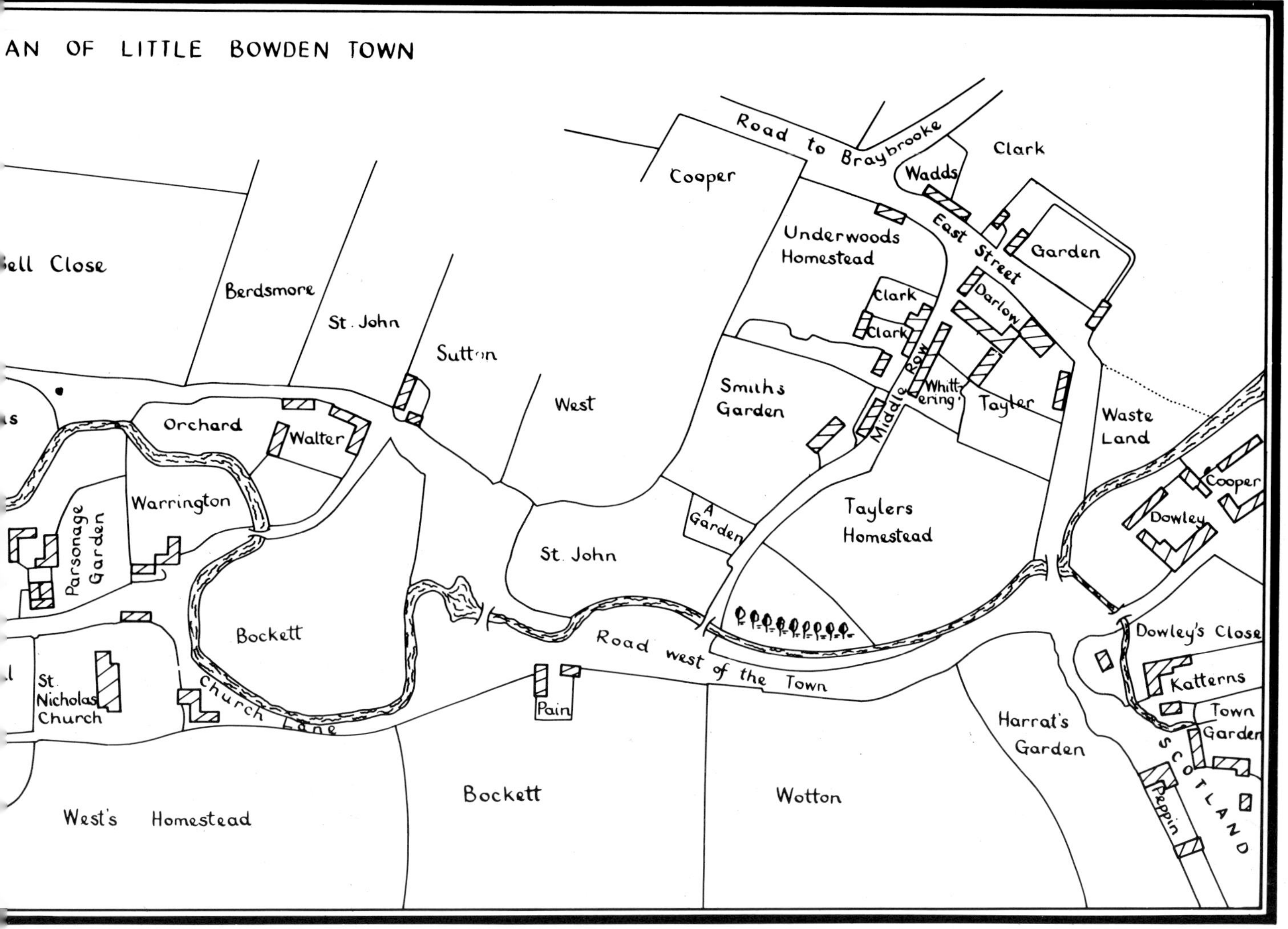

This plan of Little Bowden is based on an old map drawn after the field enclosures of 1780 and shows a strong similarity to the same area as it is today.

Braybrook Road is shown as East Street, Queen Street was Middle Row and Scotland Road the Road West of the Town.

Great Bowden parish church as depicted in 1791.

The village pond at Great Bowden in 1906, now filled in.

St. Mary in Arden

The Church of St. Mary's.

The **Harborough** parish church choir singing the Easter Hymn **around** the Hubbard gravestone for which it was paid a **guinea** (£1.05) a year.

These pictures were taken at the turn of the century.

The weekly market on the Square. During the big October fair large numbers of animals were brought into the town, sheep being accommodated on the Square or Sheep Market as it was then known.

Markets

The retail market on the Square in the mid 1930's before the stalls were transferred to the covered market hall in 1938.

In years past that part of the High Street between the Beast Market at its northern end and the Sheep Market on the Square, was an open trading area without buildings between it and Church Street. Where the Town Hall stands were Butchers Shambles, then a Corn Market and next to that a Cloth Market. Originally the Traders removed their stalls at the close of the market but gradually these emerged as shops thus forming Church Street. Dairy items were sold in the Butter Market under the Old Grammar School and pots in Church Square.

The annual fair on the Square in 1890. At the April and October Fairs the High Street, Church Square and the Square became crowded not only with traders but by entertainers and roundabouts as well as horse-drawn traffic bringing country people into the town for the event.
At the larger Fair in October, the shows would include travelling theatres with their interiors lit by gas, bands and wild animals. During the course of the Fair, which lasted nine days, farm hands were hired for the year up to the next Fair.

Cattle market in the northern end of the High Street. The beasts were kept off property and footpaths by means of chains hung between posts. Originally held on Mondays, the market was changed to Tuesday in 1221 by permission of the King to avoid conflicting with the one at Rothwell.

The original station built by the London & N.W. Railway Co. for its Rugby to Stamford line opened in 1850. It was approached from Gt. Bowden Road. From 1858 it was also used by trains to London, King's Cross, Northampton ones from 1859 and Melton Mowbray trains from 1883. It was replaced by the present station in 1884. In 1857 the 2nd class fare to london was 7/10d (39p).

Transport

Mr. Foster's boat houses on the canal at Leicester Road with rowing boats for hire. In the grounds were public tennis courts and a bowling green.

A lazy Sunday on the canal complete with sail and gramophone. The gentlemen are Messrs H, J and P. Martin, H. Foster and F. Wood.

The London to Manchester coach stopping for refreshments and a change of horses. Also shown is a covered waggon, an open cart and a pack horse.

In 1828 the following coaches called at Market Harborough on their way to London: The Royal Mail, Defiance and Express at the Three Swans; The Independent and Courier at the Angel; The Telegraph, Comet, Times and Union at the George; The Royal Bruce at the Three Crowns and the Hope at the Hind.

Two of the latest models in 1910 at the Pytchley Autocar Company's garage, Leicester Road, now the Regent Autocar Co. Ltd.

Members of a London motor cycle club outside the Angel Hotel, May 1904. The club was in the town at the invitation of their President Mr E. Kennard of The Barn, Shrewsbury Avenue who had escorted them from Newport Pagnell.

CARTERS MUSIC DEPO
WOOD
CARTE

At Work

Inside Stayne's tannery on the Commons in 1885. On one occasion a whale, cut up into sections was delivered to the works for processing and placed in the entrance to the yard so that it could be seen by townspeople.

Hunt's shop in Church Square hung with English Turkeys from 8d lb and Prime Geese from 7d (3p) lb. The Sun Inn is on the right and the entrance to the Sun Yard is through the archway on the left.

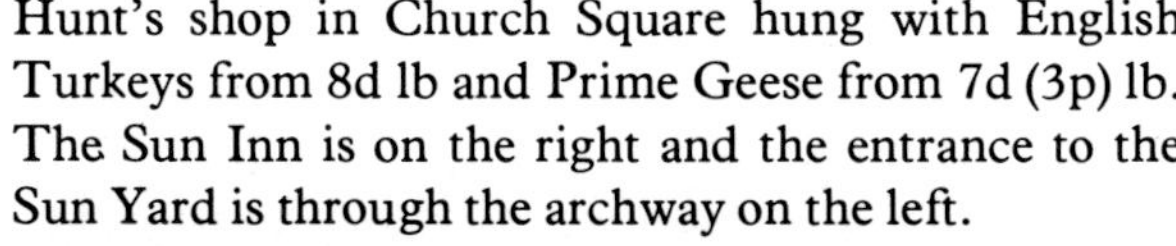

The chain bridge and ford across the River Welland, 1792. So called because a chain prevented carts using the bridge except when it was removed in times of flood.